Handy Houses
Memorize the Piano Keys
in 5 Minutes

Created, written, and illustrated by
Samantha K. Perkins

978-0-9906091-5-5
United States of America

More Love Enterprises
HomePages Books
pianifyme.com

To my little "kitty"

See the piano as a pianist sees it — remember where the letters are!

Go from this…

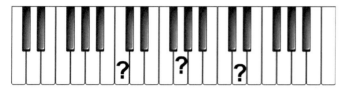

to this!

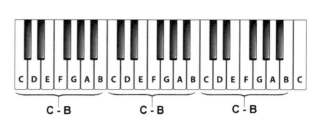

Gain a true understanding of the full keyboard with this revolutionary new method, based on an ancient memory trick.

Learn effortlessly and progress faster! It's absolutely crucial as a beginner to become very familiar with the keyboard letters. What used to take weeks or months to remember, this book will teach you in five minutes, and you will always remember it. Master the piano faster and get the most benefit from your piano lessons. This book will help you spend less time and money on lessons by covering the basics more quickly.

I am excited to share this book with you. As a piano teacher I developed this method, essentially a mnemonic device, because no memory trick existed in any method book available for learning letter placement on the keyboard. As a child I learned the old way: by "counting up" from C to remember where a letter was.

A far superior approach struck me while teaching my daughter, and this book is the result. I have tested it on adults, children with learning disabilities, current students, and people who had never touched a piano. The results were obvious: anyone can learn the Handy Houses Method, guaranteed. My students learn the keys faster, more permanently, and almost effortlessly— simply by reading this book and doing the 5-minute activity. As a result, they progress faster toward piano proficiency. This book is a must-read for anyone who is still counting up from C or has not completely mastered the keyboard letters. Don't suffer the slow way any longer. Maximize your growth with the Handy Houses Method!

There is more to Handy Houses than meets the eye — more than just assigning a picture to a letter. See the Appendix to learn the secrets of this powerful teaching tool, including guidelines and strategies for teachers.

Handy Houses

Memorize the Piano Keys
in 5 Minutes!

What do you see in this picture?
I see a **dog house** and a **people house.** I call these the

handy houses.

There is a **secret** hidden in this picture. Can you find it?

Wait, not yet!

First I have to add some more pieces to the picture.
Each piece is a clue. Then let's see if you can figure out the secret.

The first thing I'll add is a

car.

A car parks next to the doghouse. It is shiny and loud and smells like that car smell. Have you ever smelled that car smell?

There's more missing from this scene. What goes in the dog house

That's right, a dog. (That was an easy one.)

Duke the dog lives in the doghouse next to the car. When he hears the car pulling up, he barks with delight. He knows his master is home. He can smell that car smell, too.

But what does Duke the dog see wandering into the yard?

Go on, take a guess.

An elephant?! What's an elephant doing in the yard? Did she escape from the circus or the zoo? A little elephant named Ellie happily stomps over, right next to the dog house. Duke the dog can see her… and smell her.

Do you think Duke is scared?

Is he excited to have a new friend?

I'll let you decide.

Ellie the elephant notices something else in the picture, growing alongside the house…

Ellie admires the colorful flowers growing in the flower bed next to the house. The flowers are another clue.
Will she trample on the flowers?
Water them with her trunk?
Smell them?
I'll let you decide.

Someone planted these flowers next to the house,
and someone has been taking care of them.
But who?

Grandpa! It's Grandpa's flower bed. He pops his head out the window to see what the fuss is about. He can see the elephant next to his flowers, and boy does he look grumpy. Grandpa waters his flower bed every morning, and bends down with his cane to smell the flowers in the cold morning air.

What is Grumpy Grandpa thinking?
I'll let you decide.

Living in the house with Grandpa is Aunt Alice.

Not an ant… an *Aunt*. Do you have an aunt?

Aunt Alice is very kind. She takes care of Grandpa, and her room is on the other side of the house.

Aunt Alice sees something outside her window. What is it?

This is the last clue. Are you paying attention?

A **big** bumblebee!

Aunt Alice looks out her window and sees a bumblebee buzzing in the sunshine.

Now, here is what the clues mean.

Let's go through the story again… and this time, think of each clue in the story as a **piano key**.
Each one is a letter… and you just learned them all!

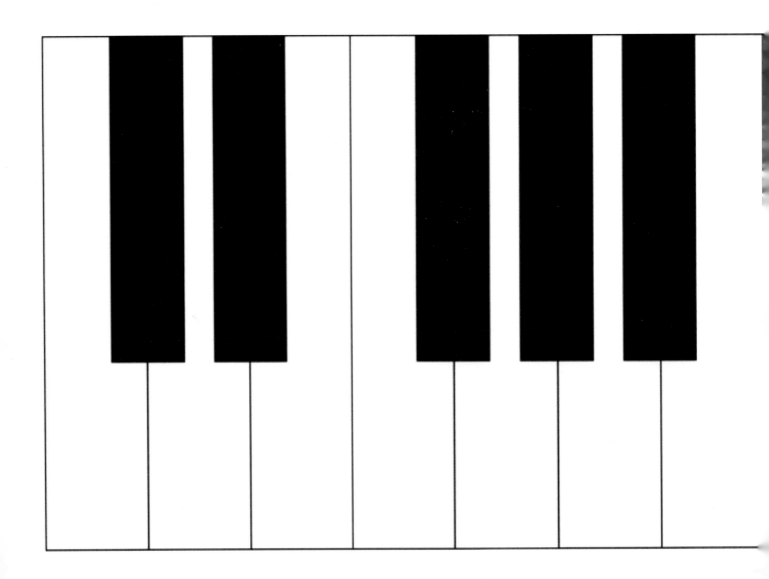

Pianos have white and black keys, and the black keys are grouped in sets of 2 and 3. These are the **handy houses**. Let's put roofs on them and use our imaginations.

Now you can see that a **set of 2 is a dog house,** and a **set of 3 is a people house**.

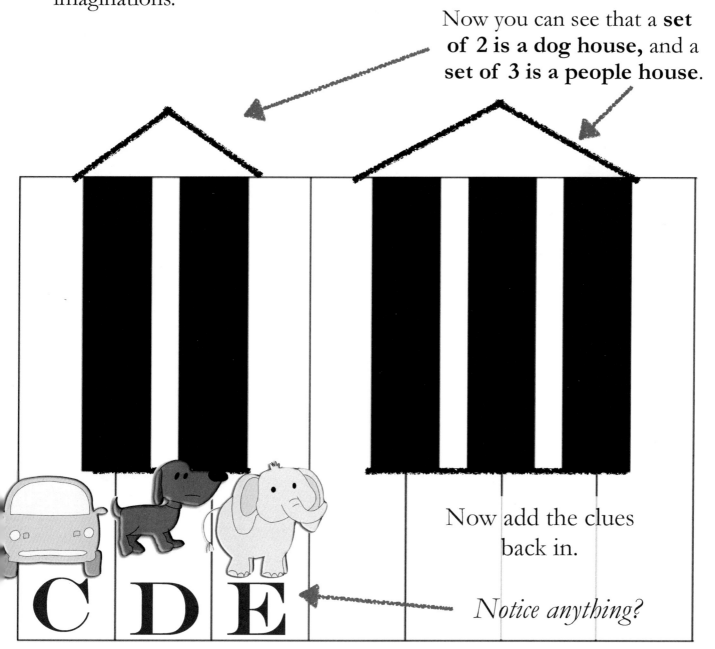

Now add the clues back in.

Notice anything?

C D E

That's right, each clue starts with a letter of the alphabet.
C for car, D for dog, and so on.

Piano keys go A B C D E F G, and we start our mental picture on the letter C.

C D E F G A B

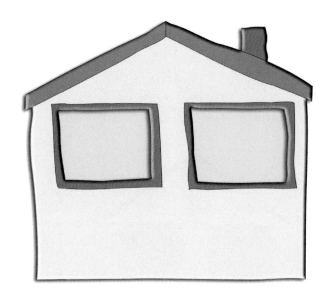

So do you remember the story? Draw your *own* clues to complete the Handy Houses picture. Remember—dogs go in dog houses, people go in people houses, and other animals belong outside. Go ahead, try it.

If you remember the story, **congratulations—you now know all the letters on the piano keyboard!** The keyboard repeats this pattern of sets of 2 and 3 black keys over and over… so you can use this picture on any part of the keyboard. Kind of like seeing a whole neighborhood of dog houses and people houses. Try it on your piano.

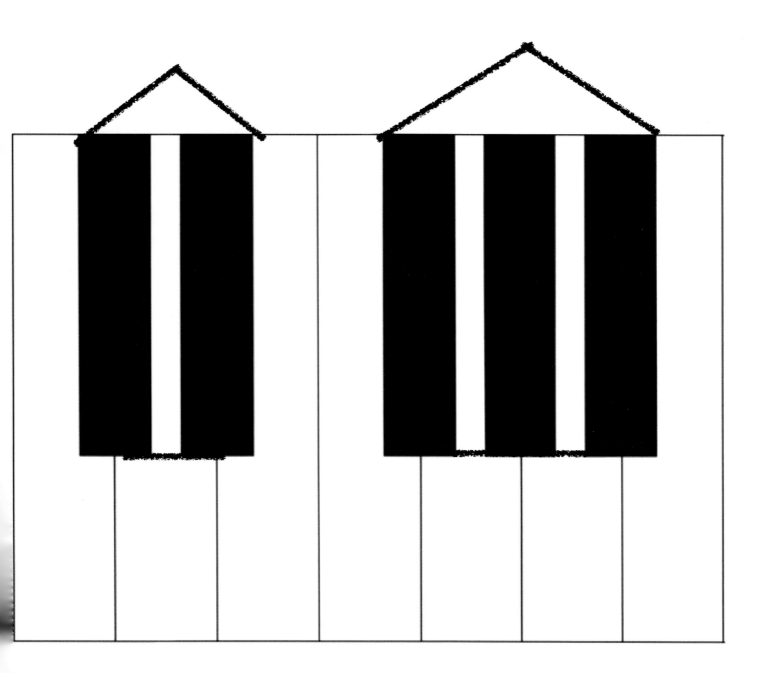

Appendix

Why do we need the Handy Houses Method?

Handy Houses is a revolutionary new mnemonic device for memorizing the placement of keys on the piano keyboard. A full keyboard consists of 88 keys repeating the letters A through G. To the untrained eye, a piano may look like a row of indistinguishable black and white keys. Without this method, beginners have to learn one letter at a time. I've found that many students learn just enough to fake it, counting up from C to find the right letters. This holds a beginner back from a comprehensive understanding of *all* the keys, and from progressing faster.

It's crucial as a beginner to become very familiar with the letters of the keys in order to become a better, faster, more educated player. Until now there did not exist a method for memorizing the letter keys. One simply had to get familiar with them over time, or expend much effort to memorize them one by one. Lesson time was devoted to learning the letters, and many students found it boring or difficult. I realized they needed a better way. Inspiration struck me at home during a lesson with my then-6-year-old daughter who was making great strides in sight-reading and music theory but still had difficulty remembering the keys.

Since the invention of the piano there have been various teaching aids developed for specific parts of one's musical education. Mnemonic devices such as "Every Good Boy Does Fine" and The Circle of Fifths are two examples of the powerful tools others have developed and shared with the world. They are taught universally because they have proven to be incredibly useful ways of retaining that information. There exist on the market today many method books training students in the fundamentals of piano and music theory. But none of these books contain any technique or trick for remembering the letter locations. And since necessity is the mother of invention, I came up with my own technique.

The various piano books available today teach students to begin finding the letter keys on the keyboard, a few at a time, separately. Young students especially have a hard time grasping the concept. I now teach all the keys simultaneously in the very first lesson with Handy Houses. They learn instantly where the keys are in relation to the grand picture, and in relation to one another (the black keys, which key is to the right, etc.). Students who use Handy Houses can do all this without much thought, because the information is burned into their minds in a unique and visual way.

With this book and the accompanying activity, students don't have to try very hard to memorize the letters. Memorization comes naturally and almost immediately. That's the beauty of it all! Students will remember the letters' locations independently of one another, forward and backward, in any order, not relying on middle C as a crutch or counting up the alphabet.

How does it work so effectively?

The story and technique are based on research, psychology, and personal experience with students. In learning about memory I came across two age-old methods for remembering a list of items: the Link Method and the Loci Method. As I studied these powerful concepts, I realized I could apply them in my teaching. Memory champions, Vegas card-counters, great orators, and illusionists are among the many who find these techniques invaluable.

The Method of Loci, or Memory Palace, dating back to ancient Rome and Greece, involves creating a vivid mental scene in which to place objects you wish to remember. It is useful for storing vast amounts of information. The Link Method is for remembering a list of items and its magic lies in the interaction of each object with the ones before and after it, thereby linking them in a memorable way. I combined the strategies of using a PLACE to fill with objects, and LINKING in a way that involves senses and emotions, and from those was born the Handy Houses mnemonic device.

This technique is effective due to sensory involvement, linking, and location. The houses are most important because they create a visual context for each object (letter). Handy Houses is kinesthetic (student draws), visual (student sees), and audible (student hears the story and repeats it back). This makes it suitable for everyone, as we all have our own learning strengths.

Instructions For Teachers

After reading the rest of the Appendix, teachers can use these guidelines I compiled as I further developed my teaching approach. Use the following strategies to ensure maximum effectiveness with Handy Houses.

The Drawing

Make copies of the keyboard page (or download the PDF on pianifyme.com) for each student. Students will draw each object (car, dog, elephant) in the scene on the corresponding key, remaking the story after it's been read.

Linking each object to both objects beside it is a crucial part of this visual memory system. Details in the story such as "the dog can see and smell the car" or "grandpa bends down to smell the flowers" are the links. You can ask additional questions using the senses about each picture if the student is younger or newer, or you can skip the fluff for adult students. Sensory details will enhance the memory. If you can get the student to feel emotion about any of these objects, even better. For instance, I ask if the student has ever had a dog, and ask for details about it while the student draws on the D key. I ask, "Have you ever smelled an elephant?" to invoke a smell memory.

Let the student know their drawings don't have to be perfect or complex; my students enjoy laughing at their elephant drawings! It's only important that it looks like an elephant to the artist. Make sure they can "see" each object drawn, that they can tell the difference between their dog and their elephant.

The book gives the students options in the story: Will the elephant trample the flowers, or water them with her trunk? This involves the student in the creative process, making the story that much more memorable. Even from mentioning the two options, many students remember both later on.

When asking them to draw Grandpa, offer glasses, a bald head, and a cane as indicators (we don't want them thinking it's "D for dad" or "B for brother"). To indicate Aunt Alice not being just a "girl" (which will make them think of G), ask the student to draw their own aunt.

Reiterate that this is all easy to remember because it's logical—people go inside the house, dogs go in dog houses, and elephants don't belong inside. Flower beds naturally go along the side of a house. People houses are bigger (wider) than dog houses.

It's important to remember that Grandpa comes before Aunt on the piano. So be emphatic when linking Grandpa to Flowerbed and Aunt to Bee. Point out that bee wings can look like B's. It's an unusually large bee; maybe its buzz is very loud and distracting to Aunt Alice. Maybe she likes it; maybe she's scared. Involve the imagination in your process.

Occasionally a student will think of an alternative object for that letter, but I recommend not changing anything. For instance, using all animals would make remembering the order of them quite difficult. Putting a Giraffe in the house instead of Grandpa would throw students off. One thing that *can* be changed if desired is the B—as long as Aunt Alice can look out the window at the object and you can somehow link her to it, feel free to use an alternative such as a butterfly, ball, bike… all things that could be on the side of a house. Additionally, don't add other details or objects into the picture. Giving Duke the dog a ball or bowl may cause the student to think of B instead of D. We want to keep the picture very simple so that students can memorize the seven items in order without effort.

Reinforcement

When the student is done drawing, ask him or her to briefly recount the story using their own drawing. The student will remember everything, including many sensory details. Having them summarize the story and "teach" it to the teacher enhances the memory process.

Immediately test whether the student has absorbed the information. Use the real piano now (without the images in sight) and point out (or ask them to point out) the dog house and the people house. Have the student identify the right key as you ask a few review questions like "Where was the flower bed planted? What was the aunt looking at? Where is the car? What was between the dog house and flower bed?" It's also fun to ask students to play a series such as "dog-grandpa-bee".

When finished, instruct the student to color the picture at home, so that not too much lesson time is spent on this activity. They must hang it somewhere they will see it daily, so that they casually notice their own picture during the week. Additionally, students can be assigned to read the book again at home, or share the book or their drawing with a family member. Have students bring the colored picture to the next lesson and summarize the story to you once more.

I often distinguish once more between Grandpa and Aunt Alice in their respective locations (G and A are the most commonly confused keys in my experience.) I also ask them to find Bee and then Car, in that order, to ensure that they understand that the image is repeated across the keyboard.

Then switch to just asking, "Where is the D? B? A?" They will know all the keys! (Check a couple more times at subsequent lessons and you will find that they do indeed know all the keys without having to count up from C.) Test them on various octaves. You'll be amazed at how quickly they absorb this information compared to the old way! Happy teaching.

Did you enjoy learning the piano keys this way? I love hearing feedback from students and other music teachers. I developed this method just for people like us.
Please visit www.PianifyMe.com to send me an email.
If you found this book helpful please consider writing a review on Amazon or any other book review websites.

Scan QR code to visit
PianifyMe.com on your
smartphone or tablet.

Made in the USA
Middletown, DE
06 March 2019